# Liftoff

## Careers in Satellite, the World's First and Most Successful Space Industry

Researched and written by Daniel Freyer

Edited by Robert Bell and Tamara Bond

Researched and written by Daniel Freyer.

Edited by Robert Bell and Tamara Bond.

Copyright © 2012 by the Society of Satellite Professionals International
All rights reserved.
ISBN: 1466402520
ISBN-13: 9781466402522
CreateSpace, North Charleston, SC

## Acknowledgments

We would like to thank the following individuals for the generous donation of their time and expertise to the writing of this guide.

- Julie Bettinger, iDirect
- Derek Edinger, Space Systems/Loral
- Anna Fry, Harris CapRock Communications
- Chris Hoeber, Space Systems/Loral
- Jonas Johnson, Economic Research Institute
- Valierie Junger, Space Systems/Loral
- Nikola Kromer, iDirect
- Wendy Lewis, Space Systems/Loral
- Cheryl Nishimura, DIRECTV
- Melodee Paul, Keystone Enterprise Services
- Tony Roberts, Disney
- Peter Semenach, Harris CapRock Communications
- Balachander Srinivasan, iDirect

We gratefully acknowledge the support of Harris CapRock Communications for the publication of *Liftoff*.

Harris CapRock Communications is a premier global provider of fully managed, end-to-end communication solutions specifically for remote and harsh environments including the energy, government and maritime markets. Customers depend on Harris CapRock for its experience and proven capabilities including local presence in 23 countries, 1,400 employees and a robust self-owned and operated infrastructure. More information: www.harriscaprock.com

Cover photo courtesy of Arianespace.

SSPI's educational and professional development mission is underwritten by:

# Contents

# Foreword

## By Tom Eaton, President, Harris CapRock

**The very idea of building a career** in the satellite industry was a novel one almost thirty years ago, when a group of forward-thinking colleagues decided to define themselves as 'satellite professionals' and establish the Society of Satellite Professionals International (SSPI). Since that time, the satellite industry has grown significantly and afforded many professionals, including myself, with exciting opportunities and life experiences that others outside the satellite sector could only hope to be part of.

Today, our industry employs a few hundred thousand individuals and yet there is no guide, no publication that deals with careers in satellite. Although there are excellent books about the history of our industry, and a constant stream of information on technological and business developments, no materials exist that are focused on career opportunities in this exciting field. Until now.

The idea for this project came as a result of industry leaders who focused their time and efforts on one core mission to promote career development in the satellite sector. It was decided that more needed to be done to encourage college and post-graduates to learn about the rewarding opportunities that satellite offers.

The task for the writers was this: highlight a diverse group of functional career paths – from engineering, to sales, to marketing, to operations – and include a variety of industry perspectives and stories. If this toolkit succeeds in its mission, it will spark the imagination of potential industry newcomers and start them on a journey toward pursuing career options in the satellite industry.

While this new publication is designed to help beginning professionals understand the types of career opportunities that are available, we hope that even seasoned professionals will find it interesting and informative. *Liftoff's* "industry primer" section gives an excellent introduction to the landscape of companies in different parts of the industry. Professionals in a variety of roles share personal experiences, insights and lessons learned, offering thoughtful advice on what has helped shape their career successes. You will also learn how they got their start and what they enjoy about their work.

This publication owes thanks to many. The support of SSPI's board of directors, national and chapter leaders, and volunteers made this possible. The toolkit's editor and SSPI Executive Director, Robert Bell, along with principal author and researcher Dan Freyer, have done an excellent job covering the galaxy of satellite careers in just a little space. Thanks are also due to all of the organizations noted in the acknowledgments and the interviewees who generously shared their time in contributing to this project.

On behalf of Harris CapRock Communications and its team of dedicated satellite professionals, some of whom have contributed to this publication, I am honored to be associated with *Liftoff*. Harris CapRock is deeply committed to the future of this industry and to the goal of ensuring that the industry and its customers will have access to the best possible workforce in the future.

*Mr. Eaton is President of Harris CapRock Communications, Harris Corporation's global communications services business. Previously, as global operations officer for Harris CapRock, Mr. Eaton was responsible for all aspects of service delivery on a global basis and ensuring the highest quality customer experience. Prior to this role, he served as president of the business's government division, where he tripled its annual revenue between 2008 and 2011. Mr. Eaton also held key positions with G2 Satellite Solutions, a subsidiary of PanAmSat, Intelsat, as well as a co-founder or Integrated Network Services, Inc.*

# 1

# Using Satellites Every Day

Watch TV? Pay by credit card to fill up your car, or to buy stuff at a store? Navigate with a GPS unit in your car or built into your phone?

Every one of those applications uses satellite to do the job. You don't notice because the spacecraft are so far away, they are not even a dot in the night sky. You have probably seen satellite antennas on homes and commercial buildings, or maybe passed a teleport with multiple antennas pointing to satellites orbiting the earth 22,500 miles or 36,200 kilometers away. And with each passing year, those distant satellites are having a bigger impact on life here on Planet Earth.

■ Every television program you see has spent time on a satellite, whether you watch it on satellite TV, cable, over the air or on your computer or mobile gadget. Satellites are part of the core network that distributes programming and advertising around the world.

■ Every computer network, including the ones that run the Internet, gets the correct time from the Global Positioning via Satellite (GPS) system that the US Air Force put into orbit. That's how networks stay in synch all around the world.

■ Speaking of the Internet, people around the world depend on satellites to connect at broadband speeds, because satellites can reach places that are too expensive to wire up. As the Internet goes really mobile aboard ships, trains and airplanes, only satellite can keep up.

■ When hurricanes, earthquakes and other natural disasters strike, satellites are the communications lifeline that saves lives. After Hurricane Katrina in the US Gulf Coast, the Red Cross sent volunteers into the field with handheld computers. They gathered data on the emergency, marking each note with its location obtained from GPS. They uploaded the data over a satellite link to the Red Cross, which worked with Google to produce online maps that emergency responders used to coordinate their efforts and get help where it was most needed.

■ When the modern military deploys, whether by air, land or sea, satellites provide their eyes and ears. Armed forces use satellites for surveillance, navigation, communications, and remote control of high-tech weapons like drone aircraft.

■ Satellites explore the galaxy and our own world. Scientific satellites like the Hubble Space Telescope survey the farthest reaches of the universe, while earth observation satellites give us the daily weather forecast, help farmers grow more food and gather data on our changing climate.

The list goes on and on. If it were not for satellite technology, the world as you know it would be a very different – and much less interesting – place.

"What I like most about working in the satellite industry is the challenge of maintaining this single point-to-multipoint transmission system and delivering our content to a large population of viewers. Working in the satellite industry and broadcast environment provides significant job gratification and satisfaction." *Tony Roberts, Disney*

## A Global Growth Industry Hungry for Talent

There is a lot of talk these days about the space business. It may be about new and cheaper ways to launch rockets. Or maybe it's about space planes like SpaceshipOne, spaceports being built in the desert, or space tourism and space hotels. It's all good stuff. But when it comes to real business in space, there is only one: the satellite business. It's the only one that makes money today and has been making money for decades.

The satellite industry generated an estimated $144 billion in sales around the planet in 2008. The *International Satellite Directory* from

## World satellite industry revenues

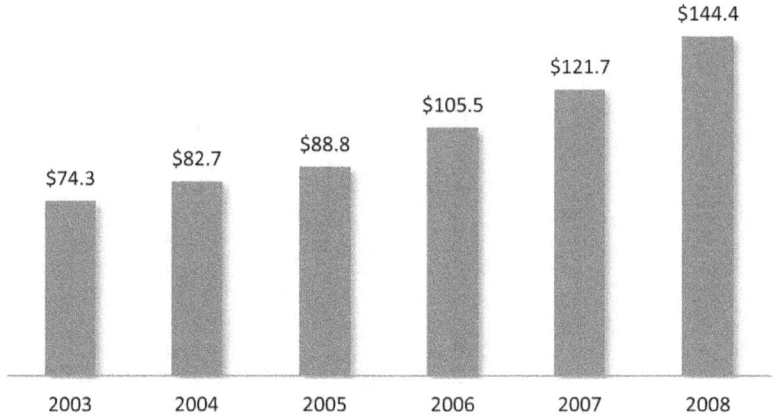

$74.3 — 2003
$82.7 — 2004
$88.8 — 2005
$105.5 — 2006
$121.7 — 2007
$144.4 — 2008

SatNews Publishers lists over 5,500 companies in its 2009 edition. And those companies are hungry for talent to feed a business that is both stable and growing, having nearly doubled in size in only five years from 2003 to 2008. Talent in engineering, communications and information technology, of course, but also management, sales, finance, marketing and many other fields. Between 2003 and 2007, the US space industry – of which the satellite industry is a part – added about 12,000 jobs. According to a study published by the Satellite Industry Association (SIA) and Futron, the U.S. satellite industry added more than 2,000 jobs between 2006 and 2007, led by satellite services employment growth of 21 percent.

In the pages that follow, you will learn about the kinds of companies that make up the satellite industry, the major employers, and the career paths they offer. We will also tell you about the industry groups, events, news media and recruiters that help you get inside the business and learn more.

# 2

# Getting to Know the Industry

A wide range of business, entertainment and government applications make use of satellite technology. Here is what they do with it.

| What are satellites good for? | | | |
|---|---|---|---|
| **Voice/Video/Data Communications** | **GPS/Navigation Position Location** | **Earth Imaging/ Remote Sensing** | **Direct-To-Consumer** |
| • Rural Telephony<br><br>• News Gathering & Distribution<br><br>• Internet Trunking<br><br>• Corporate VSAT Networks<br><br>• Tele-Medicine<br><br>• Distance Learning<br><br>• Mobile Telephony Videoconferencing<br><br>• Business Television<br><br>• Broadcast and Cable Relay<br><br>• VOIP & IP Multimedia | • Timing<br><br>• Search and Rescue<br><br>• Mapping<br><br>• Fleet Management<br><br>• Security & Database Access<br><br>• Emergency Services | • Pipeline Monitoring<br><br>• Infrastructure Planning<br><br>• Forest Fire Prevention<br><br>• Urban Planning<br><br>• Flood and Storm Watches<br><br>• Air Pollution Management<br><br>• Geospatial Services<br><br>• Security and Surveillance | • Broadband<br><br>• Satellite Television<br><br>• Satellite Radio<br><br>• Interactive Entertain- ment & Games<br><br>• Video & Data to Handhelds |

Source: Satellite Industry Association Report, www.sia.org.

The industry includes companies across the value-chain that deliver services to support these applications. Here are the major segments of the market. The chart on page 9 lists the major companies in each segment.

## Satellite Operators

The original concept for satellites – first documented by science fiction writer Arthur C. Clarke – was a set of communications "space stations" in orbit. Communications is still the largest part of the business, and the largest service providers in the industry are the owners and operators of satellites in orbit. They fall into two categories:

■ **Fixed Satellite Services** (FSS) provide video, voice and data communications to fixed locations, whether it is people's homes, rural telephone companies, gas stations or military bases. The top FSS companies worldwide are Intelsat, SES Global, Eutelsat and Telesat. Newer players include Wildblue, Hughes and ViaSat.

■ **Mobile Satellite Services** (MSS), which provide communications to ships at sea, airplanes in flight, moving vehicles on land and people on the move. The top MSS companies around the world are Inmarsat, Globalstar, Iridium and Thuraya. Newer players include Terrestar, Skyterra and ICO Global Communications.

## Spacecraft and Rockets

Major companies in the industry manufacture satellites and launch them into space. Some companies do both. It is an extremely high-tech and high-risk business, because each satellite represents an enormous investment of money and time.

■ **Spacecraft Manufacturers** take specifications from a satellite operator and, in a highly collaborative process, turn them into a functioning spacecraft able to survive the pounding of a rocket launching and serve 15-20 years in high Earth orbit. Major manufacturers include Boeing, Orbital Sciences, Northrop Grumman, Space Systems/Loral, Alcatel, EADS Astrium, Lockheed Martin and Northrop Grumman.

■ **Spacecraft Component Suppliers** are vendors to the companies that engineer and manufacture whole satellites. There are thousands of such engineering and manufacturing companies around the world. Global leaders include Ball Aerospace, Aeroject and ComDev.

■ **Launch Service Companies** receive the satellite from the manufacturer and take responsibility for putting it into orbit in working condition. Major launch service companies include Arianespace, International Launch Services, Orbital Sciences, the United Launch Alliance and newcomer SpaceX.

■ **Launch Vehicle Suppliers** develop the rockets, with their complex engines, guidance and control systems. Major providers include Aerospatiale, Boeing, Alenia Aerospazio, Aerojet, Surrey Space Systems, Orbital Sciences, Lockheed Martin, Khrunichev and EADS Astrium.

"Satellite technology is an integral part of government and military communications as a whole and is necessary to complete the communications chain around the globe. As an engineer, it has been inspiring to see the new technologies that use satellite communications. Google Earth and GPS are examples of how the technology can evolve. GPS used to be military, but it is now taken for granted by everyone. That continual renewal and innovation is what's exciting about this industry to me."

*Peter Semanach, Harris CapRock*

## Ground Hardware and Software

Satellite owner/operator companies typically rely on other companies to provide services using the bandwidth (or capacity) their satellites provide, and to supply and service the ground-based equipment ("or ground segment") used to communicate with satellites.

The ground-based technology used to transmit and receive signals represents about 28% of the market pie in the satellite industry, according to SIA figures. It grew an estimated 34% in 2008. Players in this field include antenna manufacturers, communications hardware and software equipment manufacturers, and related technology suppliers and service companies.

■ **Consumer Satellite Equipment.** Direct-to-home satellite services such as DIRECTV and DISH in the US rely on consumer electronics manufacturers including brands such as Sony and Thomson for the supply of hardware for their consumer satellite receiver and set-top-box systems. Leading manufacturers of this equipment around the world include Thomson, Coship, EchoStar, Homecast, Humax, KAONMedia, Pace, Samsung, TechniSat and Altech UEC. Key semiconductor suppliers include ALi, Broadcom, NEC, NXP, STMicroelectronics and Zoran. A third group of suppliers offer high-cost satellite phones for Inmarsat, Iridium and Globalstar, as well as low-cost GPS systems for cars, boats and private aircraft.

■ **Business and Data Communications Equipment.** Companies and institutions like hospitals often rely on networks employing VSAT technology (very small aperture terminal) supplied by leading companies such as Hughes, Gilat, iDirect and others. The biggest VSAT users are retail stores, banks and branch office networks, oil and gas companies, and the cell phone industry, which uses satellite to connect their towers in remote areas. One of the latest applications is the delivery of video advertising – called digital signage – to stores and malls.

■ **Broadband Terminals.** Hughes and ViaSat are leading manufacturers of broadband Internet terminals, as well as the communications suppliers of Internet-via-satellite service. The HughesNet and Wildblue services reached an estimated one million US customers in 2010, and growth continues to accelerate. They offer broadband in places where wired DSL or cable modem service is unavailable or very costly.

■ **Broadcasting Equipment Suppliers.** Comtech Radyne, Ericsson, Cisco, Harmonic, Inc. and others supply the specialized video encoding, processing and transmission hardware and systems for satellite broadest, news, cable television and direct-to-home applications.

In addition to the hardware manufacturers, an even larger number of firms provide local satellite antenna and equipment installation and maintenance. These companies employ trained technicians to install and service consumer satellite equipment at your home, broadband satellite terminals at rural businesses, and commercial VSAT-type networks at company sites around the country, or around the world. Installation businesses can even be entrepreneurial sole proprietorships.

## Ground Segment – aka Teleports

For every satellite operator with spacecraft in orbit, there are hundreds of ground-based companies that provide communications services using satellite bandwidth. They serve the global television and radio industries, telephone companies and Internet service providers, government agencies, oil and mining companies, retailers and many other businesses. They integrate satellite into complex networks involving optical fiber, microwave, wireless and mobile technologies. And they have become the world's leading experts in adapting Internet Protocol technology for satellite applications and other uses never envisioned by the developers of IP. Major teleport operators include Arqiva, Globe-Cast, Globecomm, RRsat, Encompass Digital Media, Harris CapRock and other members of the **World Teleport Association** (www. worldteleport.org).

| Who does what in the satellite industry? | | | |
|---|---|---|---|
| **Satellite Operators** | | | |
| **Fixed Satellite Services** | **General Services** | • Intelsat<br>• SES | • Telesat<br>• Eutelsat |
| | **Broadband** | • WildBlue (ViaSat)<br>• Hughes | • ASTRA |
| | **Private Networks** | • Hughes<br>• Gilat | • Spacenet |
| | **Satellite Television** | • DIRECTV<br>• EchoStar | • Sky<br>• ASTRA |
| | **Satellite Radio** | • Sirius XM Radio | • Worldspace |
| **Mobile Satellite Services** | **Voice & Data** | • Inmarsat<br>• Iridium | • Globalstar<br>• Thuraya |
| **Remote Sensing** | **Satellite Imaging** | • GeoEye<br>• RapidEye | • Spot Image |

| Spacecraft and Rockets | | | |
|---|---|---|---|
| **Satellite Manufacturers** | • Boeing<br>• Northrup Grumman<br>• Thales Alenia Space | • Orbital Sciences<br>• Alcatel<br>• Lockheed Martin | • Space Systems/<br>Loral<br>• EADS Astrium |
| **Subsystem Manufacturers** | • Ball Aerospace | • Aerojet | • ComDev |
| **Launch Services** | • Arianespace<br>• International<br>Launch Services | • United Launch<br>Alliance<br>• Orbital Sciences | • SpaceX |
| **Vehicle Manufacturers** | • Aerospatiale<br>• Boeing<br>• Khrunichev | • Alenia Aerospazio<br>• Aerojet<br>• Lockheed Martin | • Surrey Space<br>Systems<br>• Orbital Sciences<br>• EADS Astrium |
| **Ground Hardware and Software** | | | |
| **Network Equipment** | • iDirect<br>• Cisco Systems | • Harmonic<br>• Comtech EF Data | • Ericsson<br>• Newtec |
| **Satellite Antennas including VSAT** | • Cobham Satellite<br>• ASC Signal<br>• AAE Systems | • Patriot Antenna<br>• Rockwell Collins<br>• iDirect | • Motosat<br>• ATCi<br>• ViaSat |
| **Systems Integration** | • Globecomm<br>Systems | • Telecommunica-<br>tions Systems | • Harris CapRock |
| **GPS Systems** | • Gamin | Magellan | • TomTom |
| **Satellite Television** | • EchoStar | | |
| **Satellite Phones** | • Ericsson | Qualcomm | • Telit |
| **Satellite Radio** | • Pioneer | Sirius XM Radio | |
| **Ground Segment** | | | |
| **Teleport Operators** | • GlobeCast<br>• Arqiva Satellite &<br>Media<br>• Stratos Global | • Harris CapRock<br>• Globecomm<br>Systems<br>• MTN | • RRsat<br>• Telecommunica-<br>tions Systems<br>• Emerging<br>Markets Com-<br>munications |

# 3

# Getting a Job in the Satellite Industry

What are the opportunities in satellite? How good is the pay and what kinds of careers are available?

According to the U.S. Bureau of Labor Statistics, the U.S. space industry (of which satellite is a part) employs more than 262,000 men and women in 41 states including the District of Columbia. From 2003 to 2007, the US space industry added 12,000 jobs. According to a study by the Satellite Industry Association, the year from 2006 to 2007 saw the US satellite industry add 2000 jobs, led by satellite services employment growth of 21 percent.

**Please select the job title/description that most closely reflects your own**

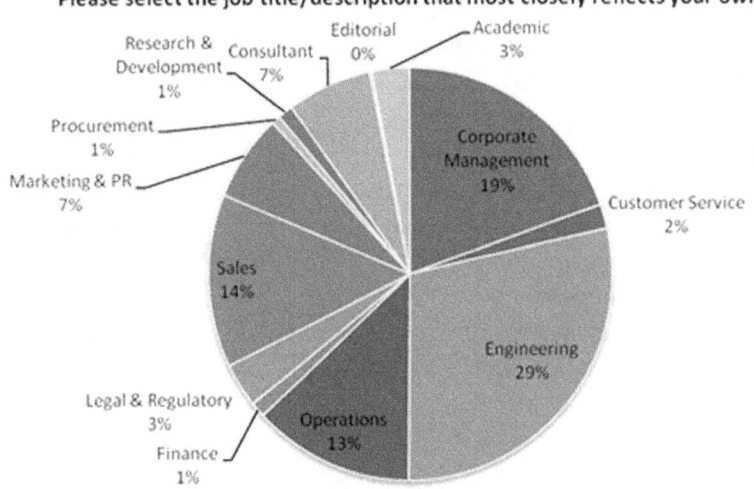

The European space industry employs another 30,000. The 30 nations that make up the Organization of Economic Cooperation and Development (OECD), which includes the US and most European nations, reported space systems and rocket manufacturing employment of 120,000 in 2006. The European space industry alone employs about 30,000, and 70% of the jobs are clustered within the four biggest European space industry firms.

## Who Does What?

The satellite industry is technology-driven, no doubt about it. According to a 2009 study by SSPI, nearly 30% of all employees work in engineering, with corporate management following at just under 20%, sales at 14% and operations at 13%. A 2009 report by the Space Foundation notes that the employment levels for aerospace engineers in the US needed to sustain anticipated activity will be 10% greater in 2016 than a decade earlier — as engineers who joined the workforce in the preceding 30 years retire. Other career paths include marketing and public relations (7%), customer service (2%), and legal & regulatory (3%).

**Employment by country in Europe by space market segment**

| Country | Launchers | Spacecraft | Ground |
|---|---|---|---|
| Austria | 47 | 254 | |
| Belgium | 340 | 751 | 193 |
| Denmark | - | 16 | 151 |
| Finland | - | 77 | 76 |
| France | 2,749 | 8,692 | 201 |
| Germany | 1,686 | 2,822 | 454 |
| Ireland | 14 | 27 | 1 |
| Italy | 425 | 2,900 | 659 |
| Luxembourg | - | 26 | 1 |
| Netherlands | 40 | 304 | 116 |
| Norway | 54 | 82 | 119 |
| Portugal | - | 34 | 75 |
| Spain | 304 | 787 | 1,004 |
| Sweden | 119 | 522 | - |
| Switzerland | 550 | 193 | - |
| United Kingdom | 9 | 3,073 | 355 |
| **Total** | **6,337** | **20,560** | **3,405** |
| **Grand Total** | | | **30,302** |

*Source: www.eurospace.com, ASD-Eurospace, facts & figures, 13th edition, rev 1. July 2009, p. 15.*

## Getting Paid

Generally speaking, the satellite industry pays well. A 2006 study by The Space Foundation reported that wages for space industry jobs are more than double the US national average wage for the private sector. Space industry jobs paid an average annual salary of $88,092 in 2007, roughly double the average salary of US professionals in the private sector, where the comparable wage, was $42,405 in the private sector. The table to the right shows average annual space industry wages by sector in the US, based on a survey performed in 2006.

**Average US space industry wages by sector**

| | |
|---|---|
| Guided missile/space vehicle manufacturing | $97,891 |
| Satellite Telecommunications | $82,998 |
| Other guided missile/ space vehicle parts | $76,760 |
| Space vehicle propulsion units/parts manufacturing | $70,054 |

Source: The Space Foundation, 2006 data.

■ The top five states in terms of space industry average annual wages are the District of Columbia, Maryland, Colorado, Massachusetts, and Virginia, based on 2007 data. All five regions had average wages exceeding $100,000.

**European salaries**

**Guided Missiles/Space Vehicle Manufacturing**

| Mean Salary | Work Experience | |
|---|---|---|
| | 1 Year | 10 Years |
| France (Euros) | 42,385 | 66,166 |
| Italy (Euros) | 32,904 | 51,429 |
| UK (Pounds) | 28,960 | 45,298 |
| US (Dollars) | 58,152 | 90,675 |

■ The top five metropolitan areas in terms of space industry average annual wages are Boston, Denver, Dallas-Ft. Worth, the Los Angeles-Long Beach metro area, and the San Jose-Sunnyvale metro area. Salaries

**Broadcasting/Wireless Communications Equipment (including satellite antennas, manufacturing)**

| Mean Salary | Work Experience | |
|---|---|---|
| | 1 Year | 10 Years |
| France (Euros) | 42,402 | 66,377 |
| Italy (Euros) | 32,844 | 51,519 |
| UK (Pounds) | 28,868 | 45,338 |
| US (Dollars) | 58,297 | 91,085 |

Source: data from the Economic Research Institute (ERI) Salary Assessor; http://www.eireri.com

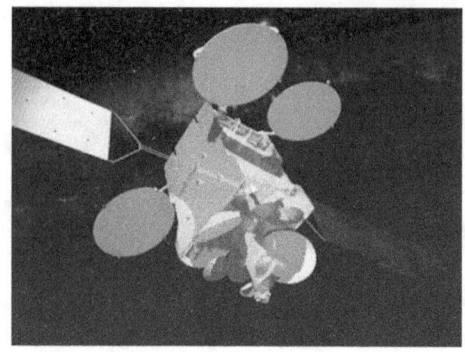

in the Boston metro area exceeded $107,000, while San Jose-Sunnyvale was the only one of the five metro areas under $100,000 at $98,552.

In Europe, salaries also tend to reflect the highly-educated and engineering-oriented wokforce and grow significantly with years of experience. European space industry employees have higher-than-average educations. Twenty-two percent have a university degree and 53% have advanced degreees, according to a 2008 survey by the Economic Research Institute.

**Hiring Snapshot: Space Systems/Loral**

A basic electrical and mechanical engineering degree opens the doors at Space Systems/Loral (SS/L) and similar firms that supply satellites and components. SS/L had 140 openings at the beginning of 2010 for positions including RF microwave engineers, antenna engineers, communications systems engineers, and spacecraft architects. "We are always looking for senior engineering talent, but few companies do what we do, so we look at all levels of experience from 2-5 to 7-12 years or beyond," says Valerie Junger, vice president of human resources.

In the heart of Silicon Valley, SS/L competes for talent with aerospace companies when recruiting for some positions. For other positions, it competes with the general high tech sector, including local companies such as Cisco, Google and biotech startups. "Some of the talent we need is very hard to find, particularly in some of our specialized engineering groups. As a result, it is oftentimes easier to hire straight from college and then train on the job," says Junger.

"Every year we are on campus at various colleges including Cal Poly, Cornell, MIT, Stanford, and Notre Dame, among others." Derek Edinger, head of a 250-plus-sized engineering group at the company adds, "We've been growing a lot in the last few years so we've been hiring everywhere from college grads to senior professionals. We recruit through other major employment websites and get resumes through referrals. We also attend job fairs and recruit on campus at key schools."

Satellite Career Appeal: "The technology is very sexy. We have a high level of excitement when, after 24 months of design and manufacturing, we launch spacecraft into orbit," says Edinger. What's more, "We manufacture it all in Palo Alto, so if you want to see the products you design being manufactured, we offer that, unlike many other U.S. tech companies, which outsource manufacturing overseas."

Hiring Snapshot: VT iDirect

Ground equipment technology company VT iDirect's largest recruiting effort is towards engineering development for hardware, software and systems testing (software quality assurance). iDirect has hired close to 20 new employees in the last few years, "and they have made a significant impact," says Chandler Ames, Head of Recruiting, and Manager of Worldwide Staffing. Global supply chain management and marketing functions for junior staff have also been in demand.

"About 45% of hires are referrals from individual employees through our referral program. Employees refer folks they know, trust and think would work well in the company," says Ames. "We also use job-specific and industry-specific search sources in areas such as marketing and supply chain management. Examples include sites such as LinkedIn and Satllitetoday. com." iDirect also recruits through regional universities and colleges, job postings, and job fairs for junior engineering staff.

Compensation: "We look at the high tech sector, companies such as Dell, Cisco, etc. to see what they pay, and we benchmark from there. We normally pay greater than the average in the industry. We have a very competitive benefits program with 401K, health and medical benefits."

# 4

# Career Paths in the Satellite Industry

What kind of career paths are open to you in the satellite industry? Despite being a tech-driven business, it's not just for math majors and engineers-in-training. The following is a snapshot of careers in the business.

## Engineering Careers

Satellite industry engineers provide engineering support for satellites and ground systems. They are generally trained as electrical, mechanical or aerospace engineers and often specialize in systems, RF, antenna, propulsion or electrical engineering.

*Typical Requirements:*

- B.S. for most positions; however, some employers may prefer a Master's degree.
- Must be detail-oriented and analytical, with an understanding of spacecraft subsystems, satellite communication systems, spacecraft operations and ground control systems.
- May require excellent computer skills and the ability to write software programs, as well as strong written and verbal communication skills.
- Engineers working for defense contractors typically must be able to obtain security clearance.

**Satellite Manufacturing.** Aerospace engineers working for satellite manufacturers develop specifications for the multiple systems that make up a satellite in order to accomplish the objectives set by the satellite owner. They create designs based on those specifications and oversee assembly, testing and the constant problem-solving required to meet the objectives within the strict design limits of a spacecraft. Engineers typically specialize in one or more of the major systems, from propulsion and power control to antennas and radio-frequency systems.

## Building Satellites: Executive Job Profile

**Chris Hoeber, Senior Vice President of Program Management and Systems Engineering, Space Systems/Loral**

Space Systems/Loral ("SS/L") of Palo Alto, California designs and builds satellites and spacecraft systems for commercial and government customers around the world. As a leading provider of commercial satellites, the company works closely with satellite operators to deliver spacecraft for a broad range of services including direct-to-home television, digital audio radio, broadband Internet and digital multimedia broadcasting. Hundreds of millions of people rely on SS/L satellites every day.

**Responsibilities:** Program-specific satellite engineering; leads an organization of 450+ people that handles spacecraft design and customer care for spacecraft programs. His group translates service requirements into a satellite and develops the requirements for all of the spacecraft hardware.

**Background:** 39 Years in the industry in satellite systems engineering, testing, and program management, building spacecraft and working with customers from around the world. Hired out of college, he was given the job of writing test software and put in front of satellites. "From day one I was exposed to an entire spacecraft - not a little widget on a table or a thing on my bench." He went on to write the test software for the world's first domestic communications satellite. To people who tell him his experience was unique, Hoeber is adamant that it is not. "You can get the same experience — you just have to look for the opportunities."

**What's Cool About Working in Satellite?** "It is fast-paced and rapidly evolving. If you have an idea or contribution to make, you can see it come to fruition in a relatively short amount of time. After two years at Hughes, I remember calling my father and saying 'Hey Dad my fingerprints are in space!" says Hoeber. "Fifty years ago, folks thought the only thing you could do via satellite was make telephone calls or broadcast television across the ocean. Today you can listen to satellite-delivered radio via the Sirius XM Radio antenna on your car; watch hundreds of channels on your TV via a DIRECTV or EchoStar dish on your roof; soon you will carry around TerraStar mobile phones that switch from terrestrial to satellite service when needed; and if you live in a rural area, you can get broadband access with ViaSat or Hughes. These are all ideas that, once upon a time, people would have said were impossible."

**A Global Industry Brings Rich International Experiences:** The chance to work with customers from all around the world on large, sometimes nationally important satellite programs, and the cultural exposure he has gained from this experience has been very rewarding to Hoeber. "I really enjoy that it's global. For satellite applications found in the U.S., similar companies around the world in Europe, Asia, Africa and the Middle East have similar applications in their regions, so there are opportunities to work in markets around the world."

**Biggest Challenges:** "Since you cannot take apart a satellite and inspect it, sometimes you have to infer things from measured performance, or telemetry to resolve issues. Sometimes I feel like a detective. It really is a forensic science to understand what is happening based on limited information."

**Satellite Launch Services.** Aerospace engineers work for launch companies to design, construct and test rocket systems and integrate them with spacecraft payloads. They may conduct basic and applied research to evaluate the adaptability of materials and equipment to launcher design and manufacture. They may also recommend improvements in testing equipment and techniques, and research and develop new technologies for use in space systems, often specializing in areas such as structural design, propulsion, acoustics, orbital mechanics, guidance, navigation and control, instrumentation and communication, or production methods. Many engineers specialize in a subsystem, and may become experts in disciplines such as aerodynamics, thermodynamics, celestial mechanics, propulsion, acoustics, or guidance and control systems.

**Satellite Operations.** Satellite operations engineers' responsibilities can include the more complex testing and analysis activities involving satellite operations (e.g., launch, early-orbit operations and anomaly support). Other responsibilities can include:

- Setting up and configuring ground communications support.
- Validating and executing orbit plans.
- Issuing spacecraft commands and monitoring and analyzing telemetry, and implementing corrective actions.
- Managing software and hardware used to operate spacecraft, detect system anomalies, degradation, or failures.
- Reporting on events and spacecraft operational data.
- Performing mission planning and scheduling, orbital analysis, archival and data processing, routine database and hardware maintenance.
- Maintaining logs, operations procedures and documentation.

**Ground Systems Manufacturing and Integration.** Ground systems engineers design and build satellite ground systems, hardware, software or complete networks. Their work focuses on specialized products for IP, video or data transmission such as modulators, receivers, multiplexors, encoders, and video or data management and transmission systems. They also become knowledgeable about manufacturing processes, quality control and cost modeling, as well as about the equipment in most common use by customers. Responsibilities can include:

- Analyzing and writing proposals, specifications, designs and/or plans for ground systems and satellite networks.
- Installing, testing and commissioning turnkey systems at customers' premises, which may be located worldwide.

- Managing complex projects on behalf of customers.
- Keeping abreast of technological developments in equipment and applications in satellite and terrestrial networking.

**Software.**  Software engineers design systems and products (operations concepts, algorithms, protocols, interfaces and platforms), such as real-time/embedded software and control center software. They may implement and test a wide range of different software and systems, and maintain and enhance existing products. Typical requirements include:

- A B.S. in Computer Science, Engineering, or Mathematics may be required.  Entry level may require some of these kinds of skills: Object Oriented methodology and technologies, C/C++, Java, J2E, Unix/Linux, real-time OS, Data communication protocols, TCP/IP, Web-based technologies, Database management systems, Software development process.
- Desired work experience may include: wireless data communications, Embedded, real-time software development, protocol development, applications development, system/network management and control, GUI development.

## Building Satellites: Executive Job Profile

### Derek Edinger, Multiplexer Products Department Manager, Space Systems/Loral

Satellites are very complex systems and require many different teams of engineers and technicians to design, build and assemble. Major subsystems alone can require 'mini-factories' within a satellite manufacturing company.  Subsystems such as multiplexers, antennas, propulsion systems, structures, power systems and others can be considered separate 'product lines', and have a whole separate production team focused on them. At satellite manufacturer Space Systems/Loral, one such mini-factory is the Multiplexer Products department run by Derek Edinger.

**Role & Organization:** Edinger manages a department that designs, tests and builds spacecraft multiplexers and filters. Multiplexers and filter systems are the part of the satellite communication payload that modifies, combines and separates signals into different channels. The department has about 60 people, including roughly 20 engineers and 40 technicians and supervisors. "We build satellite multiplexers, from working with our customers to define requirements which meet their goals, to initial design, and all the way through to manufacture, testing and integration to the satellite," explains Edinger. The department includes Electrical Engineers, Mechanical Engineers, Test Engineers and Responsible Engineers. Manufacturing area staff includes Assembly Technicians, and RF (radio frequency) Tune and Test Technicians who support different phases of production and testing.

**What's Cool About Working in Satellite?** "I like that satellite communications is a fast-paced industry with lots of new challenges. It is always on the cutting edge even though it has been around for a while so there is never a dull moment. If you think about what we do and see what our satellites do, we are working on technology that literally connects the world. That's amazing."

**How He Got There:** Joined SS/L because he "Was looking for something high-tech and technically challenging, but also fast-paced and commercial where I really understood how the technology was being used and that could positively impact people's lives." He started as an engineer then spent several years as a project lead, learning to manage and coordinate with other people and outside organizations. That led to increasingly higher project management positions, with more people reporting to him and more and more complex projects.

**Biggest Challenges:** "The nature of our work is technically challenging. We are building extremely complex machines, and we're always pushing the limits to maximize performance. Once it is launched, you can't go make repairs or upgrades on a satellite that is 22,000 miles above the earth, unlike almost any other kind of high-tech product, so we build things that are state-of-the art but also have to be extremely reliable."

**Career Options:** Future career directions for a Product Line Manager like Edinger could include increased responsibility over a larger manufacturing organization, or Program Management type roles, managing a specific satellite program from design to construction and launch.

## Information Technology Careers

It should come as no surprise that the satellite business has high demand for information technology employees, both engineers and technicians. From the design of systems in space or on the ground to the operations and maintenance of every bit of the network, IT is the glue that holds it all together.

Satellite operators and service companies that provide 24-hour real-time services need skills to design, maintain and monitor their core networks and services. Hardware manufacturers require inventory control, CRM, design, sourcing and supply chain management systems, in addition to basic administrative IT services.

Space systems suppliers, launch services providers and satellite operators require extremely sophisticated and secure systems, and need workers with skills in functions and fields such as RF engineering, video and data communications, video and data processing, telemetry, security and encryption, as well as specialized information systems.

*Typical Requirements:*

- B.S./M.S. Computer Science or equivalent, plus experience for engineering positions.
- Associates or Bachelor's in Computer Science/IT. Qualifications required can span across a wide variety of hardware, software and network skills.
- Can require knowledge in IP internetworking - MPLS (MPLS VPN, TE), IP routing protocols (OSPF, BGP, ISIS), Quality of Service (QoS), IP multicast.
- Experience with router products and software (e.g., Cisco certifications).
- May require knowledge of LAN switching protocols and security components functionality.
- May require familiarity with transport protocols and technology; experience in testing and managing equipment.
- May range from software development, programming, testing and system implementation to database administration, etc.

# Job Profile: Software Engineer

## Balachander Srinivasan, Sr. Software Engineer, iDirect, Inc.

iDirect, headquartered in Herndon, Virginia, creates satellite-based IP communications technology enabling constant connectivity for voice, video and data applications in diverse and challenging environments.

**Role:** Part of an Embedded Software engineering team that designs, develops, tests and integrates networking and control related software for the iDirect satellite broadband routers and hub line cards. Participates in determining the future direction of the Satellite Router and related products in the areas of infrastructure, redundancy, scalability and 24x7 availability. "In my function, we are writing a piece of code for a very specific device with very specific applications, so you need to choose what type of code and know how to use it. It involves not only working with external software and hardware vendors, and our hardware team, but also writing the code to solve the problem," explains Srinivasan.

**What's Cool About Satellite:** "Compared to other industries, working in the satellite industry today can be at the cutting edge of technology. It presents a lot of challenges to the engineer in terms of reducing costs, and trying to compete with the terrestrial world, but we have the advantage of being able to reach places the terrestrial world cannot."

**On The Job:** "Most of my work is spent designing our next-generation product line: our router products. A lot involves looking at what technology is out there in terms of chips, processers and how we can develop a better product. Then I go back to the drawing board and design the software."

**Background:** B.S. and M.S.E.E. A Master's thesis focused on real-time systems for satellite, gave him a feel of the industry and a theoretical technical background. Over 11 years product engineering experience including real-time embedded software, and 3 years with iDirect.

**Best Part Of The Job:** "The unique challenges that need to be solved in satellite communications and delivering broadband via satellite are a big motivator for me as an engineer. It drives you to go the extra mile."

**Career Opportunities:** The career path of a software engineer like Srinivasan may progress to managing larger teams, or expanding across more functional departments and offices, to becoming a Principal Engineer, and ultimately all the way up to Chief Technology Officer in an organization.

## Technical Careers

Engineers are vital to the success of the satellite industry but they are outnumbered by technicians who assemble and test systems, operate and maintain networks and troubleshoot customer problems.

**Aerospace Technicians.** Working with space-based systems, they work in every facet of spacecraft production: construction, testing and maintenance. Typically, they specialize in one of the areas of production. For example, using special equipment and computers, an aerospace technician may regularly assemble, calibrate and test payload, propulsion, thermal, power, control and other subsystems, or perform routine preventative maintenance.

*Typical Requirements:*
- The education of an engineering technician is not as rigorous as that of an engineer. Associate degree, or 2-year, programs in engineering technology (the preferred degree for potential technicians).
- Usually emphasize hands-on learning in a laboratory and/or 'real-world' setting.

**Teleport, Network Operations and Manufacturing Technicians.** In teleports and other ground-based facilities, technicians manage earth-to-space communications networks for video and data services, as well as spacecraft and launch tracking, and telemetry and command services (TT&C). The manufacturers of ground-based systems need skilled technicians to assemble, test, install and troubleshoot their products. The work environment is typically informal and hands-on, and can involve shift assignments, some physical labor and work outside normal business hours. Career tracks can build from operator to supervisor to management with increasing responsibilities such as:
- Installation, testing, operations and maintenance of satellite earth station equipment, and service resolution of technical issues.

- Operation and maintenance of systems including mechanical, electrical, network and RF elements.
- Customer technical support and troubleshooting.
- Maintaining equipment inventory and configuration management records, including software releases, patches, etc.

*Typical Requirements:*

- Associates Technical degree, or B.S. in Electrical Engineering (or equivalent combination of education and technical experience).
- Experience with telecommunications and/or video network technical operations, satellite gateway, wireless telecommunications, and/or CATV network operations.
- Expertise with telecom transmission facilities, infrastructure, and circuit termination equipment, LAN/WAN standards, and TCP/IP and Ethernet configuration and functionality.
- Experience with Telco and IP protocol core network and equipment, or in the case of video services, with MPEG and video transmission and encoding, multiplexing and reception equipment.
- Troubleshooting skills, e.g., ability to use and interpret readings from a range of test equipment such as spectrum analyzer, oscilloscope, protocol analyzer, power meter, etc.

## Teleport and Broadcast Operations

### Tony Roberts, Manager, Earth Station, Disney ABC Television Group

Did you ever wonder how cable TV signals get to your home? Satellites bounce it back to earth and your local satellite dish or cable TV station after an uplink earth station beams the signal up to space. Tony Roberts manages a Walt Disney Company satellite facility that beams cable network television channels, including Disney Channel, over satellite to cable stations around the country.

**Working in Satellite:** "The most rewarding part of my job is staying current on the constant changes in the technologies we use to run our business. Operating a modern broadcast facility in this digital age brings many challenges to how we deliver HD content to our affiliates over satellite. The technical complexity of our systems keeps the job interesting. I would advise a young person interested in a career in satellite communications to get the background in a small market through internships, volunteering and networking with people in our industry."

**Role: Manager in Broadcast Operations & Engineering Transmission:** Makes sure that daily operations of the transmission facility (earth station) run smoothly, and that signals meet standards and stay on the air 24x7; Manages operating staff and day-to-day issues for earth station engineering and operations; Responds, with team, to trouble calls and network outages to restore failed hardware and maintain the performance of Disney's networks; Maintains knowledge of, and proficiency with, technical equipment employed to deliver content over satellites.

**Background: From TV Operations to Satellite:** 24 years in television, starting as high school intern with his local cable company. After a first job in operations at a TV station while attending college with a focus on Radio, Television and Film, working as a technical director on live local newscasts gave him experience using satellite technology. Subsequent operations experience with a teleport that provided cable TV network uplinks led him to his current role managing Disney's uplink in Burbank, California.

**Challenges:** "Working in a live television environment taught me how to perform well under pressure where providing uninterrupted service is essential to our business," says Roberts. "The most challenging aspects of my role as an earth station manager are developing and grooming my crew to understand signal flow and the transmission systems we operate."

## Career Track: Live Television via Satellite

### Melodee Paul, Director of Special Events, Keystone Enterprise Services

Keystone Enterprise Services is a leader in satellite enterprise video, helps organizations deliver large-scale private and interactive video for corporate communications, training, broadcast and special events.

**Responsibilities:** Leads Special Events services business, which handles thousands of hours of broadcasts each year. Manages services including: remote and live satellite production; transmission of events such as major corporate and media events, news stories, major sports events and live entertainment programs.

**Background:** A respected expert in managing complete satellite production and transmission services for multiple special events and projects around the world, she has helped develop and deploy many satellite Business Television (BTV) networks for corporate, non-profits and religious organizations. In previous roles at Eventcom International by Marriott, Grey Advertising, and in TV and radio, she helped scores of leading companies produce hundreds of successful live broadcast events.

**How She Got Into Satellite:** "My background was media: television and advertising. When I moved to Utah in the 1980s, Bonnevile Satellite had an opening for what they called a traffic manager. Since I'd done that for TV and radio I was a shoe-in because at that time satellite was a new field. I stayed with it since then."

**A Day on the Job:** "Depending on the project, I'll hire a production crew and satellite trucks to go to a remote location to broadcast a show like Oprah Winfrey, or for a private corporate broadcast like HP's all-employee meeting over satellite. It could also be for news and sports events."

**Best Part of the Job:** "I work with so many different types of people and companies. You work with movie stars, CEOs of companies, reporters, news anchors and sporting figures. So it's always fun. From sports to government projects, to entertainment to companies, to news, there is so much variety that it makes for very exciting and fun work. There are always interesting things to do and it's very challenging."

## Business Careers

Space technology is cool, but at heart, most satellite businesses are just that – businesses. They need people who know how to sell, to market and to manage a complex enterprise subject to laws and regulations as well as the demands of the marketplace.

**Sales.** Selling in the satellite business requires a technical background and industry experience. Inside sales, client services and sales support positions can provide entry-level opportunities to learn about the industry and customers while developing sales skills. The career path can lead to top management.

*Typical Requirements:*
- B.A. or B.S. Business, economics, science or technical studies may be required.
- May require experience in satellite communications or telecommunications, or selling high-value, high-revenue, complex products to technical and top management.
- Typically requires frequent travel, strong verbal and written communications skills.
- Sales engineering experience may be desirable, especially for highly technical product sales.

**Consumer Marketing.** Marketing opportunities in the industry include work for consumer/mass marketing departments with Direct-to-Home (DTH) providers (EchoStar, DIRECTV, Sirius XM Radio, Sky, ASTRA, Skyperfect, WildBlue, HughesNet, etc.), whose focus is on consumer/mass market subscriber acquisition.

*Typical Requirements*
- B.A. in liberal arts, business, marketing, product management, or similar industry experience. MBA is desirable.
- Required and desired qualifications can include experience and knowledge of consumer marketing, television or radio programming, media planning, analysis and buying, advertising, on-air promotion, creative, retail merchandising strategies, consumer electronics marketing, home entertainment, online and digital consumer marketing.
- Marketing staff may perform all marketing functions within a company, or by managing outside agency vendors such as public/media relations firms and advertising agencies.

## Product Marketing

### Nikola Kromer, Director of Product Marketing, iDirect Inc.

You could say she grew up in the satellite industry. Nikola Kromer was raised in French Guiana, where her father worked for launch services provider, Arianespace, and where, as a child, she often saw rockets launching communications satellites into space. This inspired her interest in space and communications.

**Key responsibilities:** Spokesperson for a line of products; responsible for messaging and positioning products in the market; manages communications for new and existing products; provides product positioning and information for customer presentations, brochures, marketing literature, web and for trade journalists; Follows customer, market, and competitor trends to keep products positioned competitively.

**On Working in Satellite Communications:** "It is an industry that never gets boring. It reinvents itself with new technologies. It also provides mission-critical, life-saving connectivity to people. Having solutions that overcome these problems is gratifying. The satellite industry helps people in the broadcast sense to stay connected, whether it is in remote places to overcome the digital divide, to connect remote ships, or for a wide range of other applications. It is satisfying to know you are part of that."

**Background:** When she had an opportunity for a paid internship at Intelsat, the largest global satellite operator, it was a natural fit with her interests. After receiving her Master's, Kromer joined Intelsat, helping customers with purchasing satellite capacity. She progressed into a sales director position, selling satellite capacity to communications providers and users of Very Small Aperture Terminal (VSAT) systems. This led to a role in marketing VSAT solutions. "Working directly with customers on a daily basis and understanding their needs gave me an understanding of what solutions can be packaged to help meet their needs. My sales experience helped me translate their requirements into specific product requirements," explains Kromer. In 2007, she moved to iDirect.

**In This Kind of Job You May:** Work with product managers, developers and engineers to understand the product and its technical specifications; work with corporate communications, press analysts and sales teams; plan and participate in and travel to customer meetings and trade shows around the world.

**Best Part of The Job:** "Helping my colleagues as a team on the launch process of a product. Putting all the features into easy-to-understand terms that helps solve the business problem, and being able to translate that and grow the understanding of what the product's about. I like hearing the success stories of how customers have overcome challenges in their markets."

## Technical Marketing and Sales Engineering

**Peter Semenach, Director of Product Development, Government Solutions, Harris CapRock**

Harris CapRock's Government Solutions team provides telecommunications and IT solutions for defense, intelligence and government organizations. It is a business unit of global communications provider, Harris CapRock, which provides service on more than 60 satellites around the globe to customers in over 140 countries, and is the world's largest provider of fully managed VSAT services to remote and harsh environments.

**Role:** Develops satellite service products such as CommandAccess, a new end-to-end managed network service via satellite; works with engineering team to create functional and 'sellable' packages of satellite services; works with finance to perform business analysis, to assess costs, pricing and profitability; trains sales team and customers on products. "A lot of people want to be entrepreneurs. Part of being in Product Management is blending your technical expertise and entrepreneurship together to create new and exciting products that meet customer needs. So I feel like a mini-business owner within the company, and it is an interesting position."

**Background:** With a B.S. in Mechanical Engineering, and a decade of satellite industry experience, he worked in both design and sales engineering functions earlier in his career. "As I grew as an engineer, I became interested in the business side of things so I got an MBA. I wanted to create something not only technically, but something that could become a profitable business for a company." After receiving his MBA, he landed a 'classical product management' job developing new products for IP-over-satellite and enterprise networks at Loral Cyberstar. He later joined Harris CapRock in a similar role.

**What's Cool About Satellite?** "Satellite technology is an integral part of government and military communications as a whole. It is necessary to complete the communications chain around the globe. As an engineer, it has been inspiring to see the new technologies that use satellite communications. Google Earth and GPS are examples of how the technology can evolve. GPS used to be military, but it is now taken for granted by everyone. That continual renewal and innovation is what's exciting about this industry to me."

**Best Part of The Job:** "The ultimate reward is having a customer satisfied and their needs met through a product that you created."

**Global Industry, Global Experiences:** "Sales Engineer and Product Manager jobs can take you around the world working on customer projects, offering experiences that can be exciting and expand your horizons. You learn about different companies, countries and cultures."

**Business-to-Business Marketing.** Product and technical marketing managers assess customer requirements and market demand, product features and pricing, create and implement marketing strategies, create distribution channels and manage them, and support and promote technical product sales.

Marketing communications positions manage corporate branding and positioning, advertising, trade show logistics, online and event communications, and trade press communications. They perform these functions both within the company and by managing outside agency vendors such as public/media relations and advertising agencies.

*Typical Requirements*
- Technical marketing positions may require a technical degree or prior product or sales engineering experience. Experience as a

sales engineer working with customers can be a good stepping-stone to a product marketing position.

- For Marketing Communications, experience with a public relations agency is a common entry point, as are entry level in-house marketing department positions, which may prefer a B.A. in communications, English, business, mass media or similar.

**Law.** There are a lot of attorneys in the satellite business and they work on an amazing variety of issues. Communications is a highly regulated business, and satellites do it in hundreds of nations, each with its own laws. Space technologies have both peaceful and military uses, and their manufacturing, export and import are tightly controlled in many places. And then there all the normal commercial disputes between competitors. In addition to corporate law and commercial transactions, areas of specialization employed in satellite industry firms can include:

- FCC telecommunications law and policy.
- International trade and export law.
- FCC licensing and frequency coordination (for space and ground systems).
- International frequency coordination and telecommunications regulatory law.
- Television and radio program licensing.
- Privacy and censorship regulations.

**Finance.** Companies in the satellite industry have the same need for financial expertise as companies in other industries. Because they are capital-intensive businesses that tend to invest in assets with long lives, they depend on skilled financial management for success. Specific areas of focus include accounting, investing, banking, insurance and securities.

*Typical Requirements:*

In addition to the usual qualifications found in other technology industries, finance positions in the satellite industry can have these specialized requirements, depending on the type of firm:

- Security Clearance: spacecraft and launch systems employ arms-traffic-controlled and export-controlled technology.
- Ability to comply with specialized import-export regulations (ITAR in the USA) in multiple countries.

- Understanding of, and ability to apply, cost burdens and comply with Government contract auditing and accounting rules (e.g., Defense Contract Audit Agency) if employed at a government contractor or Federal agency.

## Inventing the Future: Technologist Entrepreneur

### Thomas E. Moore, Senior Vice President, ViaSat Inc.

An engineer with an entrepreneurial talent, Moore found a passion for technology has led him to an important role in the industry helping to expand satellite's broadband reach into the future.

Moore is responsible for leading the team that is developing ViaSat-1, a transformational, next generation platform for satellite broadband being developed by ViaSat, Inc. (NASDAQ: VSAT).

In the 1990s, at Cable Television Laboratories (CableLabs) a nonprofit technology development consortium of the cable industry, he played a key role in designing the DOCSIS® global standard for cable modems. He had earned an M.S. in Telecommunications Engineering from the University of Colorado and an MBA from Harvard.

Living in an 'unwired' location in the Rocky Mountains in the 1990's, Moore realized that communities like his would have no broadband services unless there was a new alternative to DSL and cable modem services. He believed strongly that satellite technology promised the best solution for bringing broadband communications of the future to remote and rural locations.

With that vision of the future, he joined with others to found a satellite company called WildBlue Communications. WildBlue pioneered the introduction of a new mass-market-affordable breed of Ka-band commercial satellite service over North America. The impact of this new technical and cost paradigm has been to help drive an order of magnitude increase in the volume of home, small office and business satellite terminals in use today – from 100s of thousands to a figure that was approaching 1 million by 2010.

Although he left WildBlue after contributing to its successful launch and financing, several years later in 2008, Moore was recruited by ViaSat, a leading supplier of Ka-band terminals that had embarked on plans for a Ka-Band satellite system of its own. In 2009, ViaSat acquired WildBlue, bringing Moore back to the organization he helped found.

**On His Job:** "It's a dream come-true for me since its obviously an extension of a vision I had in the '98 timeframe to work on the next jump in the evolution of this technology. Not only is that technology working in the US, but we're extending that vision worldwide."

## The Military Option

Every branch of the Armed Forces has a space command that buys custom-built satellite technology and uses it to connect with troops on the ground, ships at sea and aircraft in the air, as well as for reconnaissance and intelligence-gathering through space-based cameras and sensors.

Military SATCOM (as it is known) offers unique opportunities for technical high school and community college graduates, as well as university grads, to receive training in satellite systems and build high-level skills. For example, the Air National Guard offers entry-level opportunities to gain hands-on experience with the latest SATCOM systems (also classified as Radio Communications Systems), and Satellite WideBand and Telemetry systems.

The scope of military SATCON is very broad, from telecommunications to information technology, geospatial intelligence analysis and program analysis to systems development, administration and engineering. Job titles include SATCOM System Operational Manager (SOM), Program Managers for satellite terminals and satellites, and SATCOM System Experts (SSE). The Air Force is the leader in developing and flying satellites but other major satellite-related military organizations include the Defense Information Systems Agency (DISA), National Geospatial-Intelligence Agency (NGA), National Reconnaissance Office (NRO), Air National Guard, Army, Navy and Marines.

Many of the people working in the commercial satellite business got their start in the military. They gained experience in the design, procurement operations and management of satellite systems in the service of their country, and brought those skills to civilian careers in the industry.

The military loves acronyms, and most military satellite programs have names drawn from a bowl of alphabet soup. To learn more, check out some of the following major military programs:

- Advanced EHF (Advanced Extra High Frequency)
- UFO (Ultra High Frequency Follow On)
- MILSTAR 1
- WGS (Wideband Global SATCOM)
- GBS (Global Broadband Service)
- MUOS (Mobile User Objective System)

## Career Track: Military to Civilian and Commercial

### Rick Sanford, former Chief Operating Officer, Cisco Internet Routing in Space

CISCO

Sanford led a team in creating the Internet Routing In Space (IRIS) technology at the forefront of satellite communications at Cisco. He was responsible for development of Cisco's first GEO space qualified routing and modem payload, as well as its business plan and future space-ground architectural solutions. Cisco, (NASDAQ: CSCO), is the worldwide leader in networking for the Internet and Cisco Internet Protocol-based (IP) networking solutions are the foundation of these networks. Sanford came into the satellite industry as an engineer in the Air Force. He later designed satellite circuits and installed satellite terminals for the Department of State for counter-narcotics networks during the "U.S war on drugs."

"I started my career in the US Air Force as an enlisted crypto technician. Then in 1986 I decided to leave the Pentagon and went to work at the State Department as a contracting design engineer looking at ground systems for satellites. It was a great way to learn a little about satellite and radio. The design work was intriguing to me. That design work and my background with the US Air Force led me to focus on satellite."

# 5

# Career Tips from Industry Pros

How do you get started in the business? Once you get your start, how do you make sure that your career takes you where you want to go? Conversations with working men and women in the business turned up these useful bits of advice.

**Internship or Co-op Positions.** Internships are a fabulous way to try things without a long-term commitment. You get to see what a company and position is like. It also opens you up to what happens in the workplace every day versus what you do in school.

**Hands-On Experience.** "Get experience with 'hands-on' projects: whether it's a car, boat or satellite. Anything that involves teamwork is a valuable learning experience," recommends SS/L's Hoeber.

**Mentors.** Gaining a mentor can be extremely valuable. "I've had the benefit of working with very smart people and really good mentors that have taught me how to solve complex problems," says SS/L's Edinger.

**Take The Initiative.** Be interested in learning more, and new things beyond your realm of expertise. Learn as much as possible from industry magazines and external sources, as well as on-the-job. Try to lean about and follow industry players, technologies and market trends.

**Work on communication skills.** This is just as important for engineers as it is for marketing and sales. For instance, in many technical companies today, strong presentation and communication skills in an engineer can take a career farther than just job seniority. "The best idea that isn't communicated well fails immediately and a bad idea that is communicated well fails eventually," explains SS/L's Edinger, who leads a technical team of over 250 staff.

**Network.** Talk with people in the industry to learn more about what they do and whether it is something you want to pursue. This will take you further than replying to a posting on a website.

**Use professional societies and associations (like SSPI),** and industry conferences to network and learn about industry happenings. It is a great way to meet people outside your school or company.

## If Your Focus is Engineering...
Software
- Gain 'area skills', and you need the ability to analyze problems, design new things and understand how things work.
- Gain a strong background in math and programming.
- Gain deep knowledge of networking and TCP/IP because the "whole world is going towards IP."
- "For an embedded software engineer, it's important to have OS (operating systems) skills. Knowledge of new platforms that are getting bigger such as POSIX, a new standard, are helpful, and all the open source Linux, DCC, and DNU related tools," recommends iDirect's Srinivasan.

### Space and Ground Systems
- Building satellites and ground systems requires a lot of very diverse disciplines to work together. The more you can learn about the big picture and how technologies and disciplines work and interact, the better off you are as an engineer.
- Testing Jobs – The Secret Benefit: "A job involved in testing gives you hands-on exposure to the spacecraft and to the people buying the spacecraft, so it is a great way to get broad and valuable experience from the beginning," says SS/L's Hoeber.

- Advanced Degrees: For satellite engineers, earning an M.S. is highly recommended. It allows you to specialize more and opens up more opportunities for experiences that you would not be exposed to with just undergraduate studies. "The branch of Electrical Engineering called RF/Microwave engineering is key to what we do, so an M.S. or Ph.D in RF/Microwave and/or Antenna engineering, and/or experience in this field is very desirable," suggests Edinger of SS/L.

## Sales Engineering and Product Management

- A BSEE degree with a concentration in wireless communications is an excellent background for getting into the industry.
- Gaining a good understanding of the technology is extremely important, whether from an Electrical Engineering or Computer Science background.
- "The two key technical foundations of this business to understand are wireless technology, of which satellite is a part, and IP (Internet Protocol) communications, including video, data and voice," says Harris CapRock's Semenach.

**From Engineering to Sales.** Engineers who work closely with sales executives and customers to support technical product sales are commonly called Sales Engineers. They are also usually in a good position to gain the experience required to become a sales or marketing professional if they enjoy and develop selling skills. This is due to the product and customer knowledge, and the customer relationships they gain.

**From Engineering to Marketing.** A career path that progresses from engineering, particularly sales engineering, to marketing is also an option, since marketing most satellite products requires the ability to grasp technology, its use by customers, and their needs.

## If You're Not Going to be an Engineer...

### Marketing Management

- Gain a theoretical background in strategy and marketing with an MBA or marketing degree.
- "It would also be helpful to have some concentration around networking, telecommunications or IP to help you differentiate

yourself in that area as a new grad because satellite is a technical industry," suggests iDirect's Kromer.

- Identify key players in the industry and stay on top of key developments and trends in the marketplace.

**From Sales to Marketing.**  Sales experience is also useful and a possible entry path to positions in marketing management. "You get to know customer's requirements, to understand the technology and learn how to position it to customers," explains Kromer, whose career has followed this trajectory.

## Broadcast Events & Production

- For grads interested in finding live satellite TV production jobs like hers, Keystone Enterprise Services' Paul recommends internships at TV stations and channels. "Try to gain experience with live production and webcasting. The more you know, the better off you are. That means learning as much as you can about TV production, studio operations, remote transmission, fiber, satellite, satellite newsgathering, etc."
- TV jobs can be exciting, and the work environment can be informal.
- For jobs involving live transmissions and on-air operations, you must be focused, detail oriented and have the ability to multitask under pressure.
- In broadcasting and satellite operations, you must be willing to work all hours and be available at all times, so dedication and strong work ethics are vital to your success.

## Internships - A Great Way To Start

Students and grads can get hands-on experience through an internship or co-op assignment while pursuing a degree, during the summer or between studies.  Interns may be given real, hands-on work assignments involving cutting-edge aerospace technology.

Listed below are some organizations with formal internship opportunities.  Many companies also have sporadic internships depending on specific department budgets.

In addition to formal programs, some executives can create an internship opportunity for volunteer or paid work if they are convinced an intern can help their business. If you have unique talents and skills you are willing to volunteer to gain experience, don't let the fact that there is no formal internship program stop you. Make a proposal. You may be surprised at the positive a reception you receive.

SSPI chapters and SSPI can also help underwrite volunteer internships in the industry with a stipend for students. For more information, visit www.sspi.org.

**Harris CapRock** has partnered with the Mitchell Technical Institute, which is the only school in the US to offer a two-year associates degree in satellite communications, to provide internship opportunities to MTI students. You can explore other internship opportunities by contacting the head of human resources, Lisa Morley, at lmorely@harris.com or 703-752-6822.

**DIRECTV** has an internship program with over 100 internship positions in its program in recent years, most located in Los Angeles. Interns get the opportunity to use classroom training, work alongside some of the industry's most respected experts, establish networking contacts, obtain references and explore potential career opportunities within DIRECTV. All positions are paid competitive student wages. Students hired should be pursuing an academic program of study that matches the work they will do as an intern. More information is available at: www.directv.com/DTVAPP/content/careers/internship. DIRECTV looks for students in:

- Business/Economics
- Communications
- Engineering (Computer Science or Electrical Engineering)
- English/Journalism
- Finance/Accounting
- Graphic Design
- Information Technology
- Law
- Logistics Management
- Marketing/Sales
- Mathematics
- Media Production
- Supply Chain

**EchoStar:** The satellite TV provider offers one of the most comprehensive internship programs in the United States, recognized by the National Association of Colleges and Employers for many best practices in internship programs. Information on this summer program: http://www.echostar.com/Company/Careers/CollegeRecruitingInternships.aspx

**Intelsat**, the global satellite operator has occasional internships and a summer program in Washington, DC and elsewhere. (www.intelsat.com)

**Orbital Sciences** (www.orbital.com/Careers/Internships/) provides interns with competitive salaries, access to state-of-the-art equipment, training, travel reimbursement at the beginning and the end of their assignment, housing assistance, and the possibility of future employment. Typically, Orbital focuses its college recruiting efforts on the following disciplines:
- Aerospace Engineering
- Computer Engineering
- Computer Science
- Electrical Engineering
- Mechanical Engineering
- Accounting

**SES World Skies**, the global satellite operator, has internship programs – with more information at: https://jobs.ses.com/

**Space Systems/Loral**: SS/L recruits students for its internship and co-op programs, and many come back as successful full time employees. Web: www.ssloral.com/html/careers/college.html

**United Launch Alliance**: (www.ulalaunch.com/index_careers.html). ULA, the top U.S. launch service provider, hires paid summer interns from a variety of disciplines and backgrounds to work on the Atlas and Delta rocket programs.

## Lifetime Learning

A comprehensive database of educational programs and courses related to satellite technology and communications can be found on SSPI's website. We offer a free searchable online directory of undergraduate,

graduate and other _educational programs_ devoted to satellites and space. It covers institutions in the Americas, Europe and Asia. Register at _www. sspi.org_ and then search by location to find programs near you.

Another online resource of educational space programs on the web is: _http://www.spacenews.com/launch/space-directory-educational. html_

### Build a Satellite in College

According to Space Systems/Loral's Sr. VP Chris Hoeber, the traditional model for systems engineering used to be that people were hired to design a system, such as propulsion hardware. "Then they would work for twenty years and gain experience in various subsystems until they could design a whole spacecraft. That has changed. Today there are a number of universities with course materials where you learn to design a spacecraft. They can have programs or contests like the University Nanosatellite Program (UNP) that teaches people how to work as a team to design a system."

Over ten universities around the country have been involved in the program. Among the schools where SS/L has had recruiting success are: University of Michigan, University of Kentucky, Cal Poly at San Luis Obispo, Cornell, Washington University and Massachusetts Institute of Technology (M.I.T.). As a result, he says, "We're discovering that people with that hands-on interdisciplinary training can come in and hit the ground running without years of experience. When we find people with that kind of training we can give them challenging, rewarding experiences almost from the start."

_(For more information on the UNP program and participating universities, visit: http://www.vs.afrl.af.mil/UNP/_

The International Space University (ISU) (www.isunet.edu), based in Strasbourg, France, is a graduate school that offers its students a unique core curriculum covering all disciplines related to space programs and enterprises – space science, space engineering, systems engineering, space policy and law, business and management, and space and society. Offerings include a two-month Space Studies Program and one-year Masters programs.

The interdisciplinary programs include intense student research and team projects that give international graduate students and young space professionals the chance to solve complex problems in an intercultural environment. Courses are taught from ISU's central campus and at locations around the world. Since its founding on the campus of MIT in 1987, with noted author and visionary Sir Arthur C. Clarke as its first Chancellor, ISU has graduated more than 2,900 students from 100 countries, many now in senior positions with commercial and government space-related organizations.

# 6

# Learning More About the Business

We hope we have been able to give you a flavor for the business, the people and the opportunities you will find in the world's first and most successful space business. But we have really just scratched the surface. If you're ready to learn more, these resources can help.

## Associations

Several trade and professional associations offer a wealth of information, networking opportunities, contacts, training, educational, internship and job board information, and opportunities that involve the satellite industry:

- **Society of Satellite Professionals International.** SSPI is the professional development society of the satellite industry. It seeks to attract new talent into the business, help satellite professionals advance in their careers, and celebrate their amazing achievements. Today, SSPI has nearly 3,000 members in 32 countries and gratefully acknowledges the support of universities, volunteers in chapters and over 60 companies on three continents. www.sspi.org
- **Satellite Broadcasting and Communications Association.** SBCA is the national trade organization representing satellite television and related businesses. www.sbca.com/direct-dish/index.html

- **Mobile Satellite Users Association.** A non-profit organization dedicated to promoting the interests of the users of Mobile Satellite Services (MSS) worldwide. www.msua.org
- **World Teleport Association.** WTA is a trade organization dedicated to advocating for the interests of teleport operators in the global telecommunications market and promoting excellence in teleport business practice, technology and operations. www.worldteleport.org
- **The Space Foundation.** A nonprofit organization supporting space activities, space professionals and education. It conducts major events for space professionals, the National Space Symposium, and the Strategic Space Symposium. www.spacefoundation.org
- **American Institute of Aeronautics and Astronautics.** AIAA is the world's largest technical society dedicated to the global aerospace profession. With more than 35,000 individual members worldwide, and 90 corporate members, AIAA brings together industry, academia and government to advance engineering and science in aviation, space and defense. www.aaia.org
- **Satellite Industry Association.** SIA is a Washington D.C. based trade association representing the leading global satellite operators, service providers, manufacturers, launch services providers and ground equipment suppliers. www.sia.org

Outside the United States, major associations include:
- **Cable and Satellite Broadcasting Association of Asia,** based in Hong Kong, represents satellite and cable TV interests in Asia. www.casbaa.com
- **Asia-Pacific Satellite Communications Council**, based in Korea, seeks to advance the market for satellite communications in the region. www.apscc.or.kr
- **GVF/Global VSAT Forum,** based in the UK, is an association of companies involved in VSAT communications to consumers, business and government. www.gvf.org
- **European Satellite Operators Association** focuses on addressing European issues for the satellite industry. www.esoa.org

For Engineers, professional engineering societies may also be helpful resources, including:

- **SAMPE** (Society for the Advancement of Material and Process Engineering). www.sampe.org
- **ASME** (American Society of Mechanical Engineering). www.asme.org
- **IEEE** (Institute of Electrical and Electronics Engineers). www.ieee.org

## Events

Industry conferences as well as local chapter meetings of organizations such as SSPI provide excellent opportunities to network and learn about companies and jobs. Top trade events include:

- March, **Satellite Conference,** Washington, DC, www.satellite2011.com
- March, **CABSAT MENA**, Dubai, UAE www.cabsat.com
- April, **SatCom Africa,** Johannesburg, South Africa, www.satcomafrica.com
- April, **National Association of Broadcasters, annual conference,** Las Vegas, www.nabshow.com
- April, **National Space Symposium**, Colorado Springs, CO www.nationalspacesymposium.org
- June, **SATELLITE Industry Forum,** Singapore www.casbaa.com
- June, **CommunicAsia, BroadcastAsia,** Singapore, Singapore Expo, www.communicasia.com www.broadcast-asia.com and www.visit-imbx.com
- September, **World Satellite Business Week**, Paris, www.satellite-business.com
- September, **International Broadcast Convention,** Amsterdam www.ibc.org
- October, **APSCC Broadcasting and Space Conference and Exhibition,** location varies, www.apscc.or.kr
- October, **Satellite & Content Delivery Conference and Expo**, New York City, www.satconexpo.com

## Industry Press & Media

Below is a list of online and print media that cover the industry. They offer many useful online links and resources, including industry job postings.

- **Via Satellite** is a leading print publication with a focus on applications and markets for satellite communications, published by Access Intelligence. Its Web site at www.satellitetoday.com offers free and subscription-based information on the industry, including video interviews with industry executives.

- **Space News** (www.spacenews.com) offers quality journalism focused on the overall space industry as a print subscription publication and via its website. It includes news on the satellite telecommunications sector with a focus on its impact on space companies.

- **Satmagazine** (www.satmagazine.com) and sister online publication **Milsatmagazine** (www.milsatmagazine.com) provide in-depth articles from industry professionals, while sister site **SatNews** (www.satnews.com) offers up-to-date news via the web and online subscription.

- **Satellite Markets & Research** (www.satellitemarkets.com) offers online and print analysis of the industry and vital statistics. It includes video and podcast interviews with key executives from the global satellite industry, as well as a bi-monthly journal *Satellite Executive Briefing*, available free with registration online.

- **Satellite Evolution Group**, based in the UK, offers both in-depth industry coverage in print periodicals covering Asia and the Mideast, as well as free subscription newsfeeds, video newscasts and interviews via the web: www.satellite-evolution.com

## Recruiters and Job Boards

In addition to job search engines such as Monster.com, there are specialized boards used by firms in the satellite industry, including:

- www.space-careers.com
- sspi.spacejobs.com
- www.gvf.org/vsat_industry/job/index.cfm

## Company Websites/Career Pages

Company websites are one of the best resources for identifying career opportunities, as most sites have a career or jobs section. Useful online directories and lists of satellite company websites include:

- *Companies Web Directory* by the publisher of *Via Satellite* at www.satellitetoday.com/webdirectory/

- Spacenews.com provides an excellent free web directory of companies in the space business at www.spacenews.com/launch/space-directory-commercial-sites.html

- Another useful free list of company websites, organized by satellite industry segment and including a complement of companies active in Europe can be found at www.satellite-links.co.uk

- *Via Satellite's* **2010 Satellite Industry Directory**, available for purchase at www.satellitetoday.com/sid includes company contacts in the industry.

- Design Publishers' **The 2010 International Satellite Directory,** *The Complete Guide To The Commercial Satellite Communications Industry*, is another resource of company contacts available for purchase, www.satnews.com/directory.shtml

## Using Society of Satellite Professionals International Resources

For audio interviews and more information on educational opportunities, industry news, local contacts and events, as well as online social networking with satellite industry professionals, visit www.sspi.org. Become a student or professional member of SSPI and launch your career!